THE PIONEER'S INTERCESSION JOURNAL

30 DAYS TO BLAZING A TRAIL

RHONDA BRATCHER

EDITED BY
NICOLE QUEEN

VISION PUBLISHING HOUSE

Copyright © 2024 by Rhonda Bratcher

All rights reserved. Published in the United States by Vision Publishing House, LLC.

Vision Publishing House
www.vision-publishinghouse.com

ISBN: 978-1-955297-55-4 (Paperback)

This book is established to provide information and inspiration to all readers. It is designed with the understanding that the author is not engaged to render any psychological, legal, or any other kind of professional advice. The content is the sole expression of the author. The author is not liable for any physical, psychological, emotional, financial, or commercial damages, including, but not limited to special, incidental, consequential, or other damages. All readers are responsible for their own choices, actions, and results.

No part of this book may be reproduced in any form or by electronic or mechanical means, including information storage and retrieval systems, without written permission from the author, except for the use of brief quotations in a book review.

CONTENTS

Day 1	7
Day 2	11
Day 3	15
Day 4	19
Day 5	23
Day 6	27
Day 7	31
Day 8	35
Day 9	39
Day 10	43
Day 11	49
Day 12	53
Day 13	57
Day 14	61
Day 15	65
Day 16	69
Day 17	73
Day 18	77
Day 19	81
Day 20	85
Day 21	91
Day 22	95
Day 23	99
Day 24	103
Day 25	107
Day 26	111
Day 27	115
Day 28	119
Day 29	123
Day 30	127

Opening Declaration

- I declare that you are a world changer, atmosphere shifter, and climate builder.

- I declare that you possess kingdom thought patterns and language.

- I declare that you will bring reformation and revival to every atmosphere you enter that receives you.

- I declare that you dominate in the apostolic, prophetic, and strategic realms, shaping the next generation to birth vision, possess indescribable courage, and an activated faith that moves mountains.

- I declare that discouragement, loneliness, persecution, distraction, lack of support, misunderstanding, or betrayal of any kind will not derail you from your assignment.

- When tradition and religion attempt to suffocate you, your mantle will illuminate and snatch you out of its clutches.

- You will overcome any form of warfare because the Lord is with you.

- Now, I declare that you cultivate, populate, and produce in your jurisdiction.

- There is a trail that you are blazing that heaven is releasing to the earth only through you. I declare that you will create space for others who are on this path.

- You are the first of your breed, not the only one.

- Therefore, move forward with power and precision; God has already gone before you.

"The Lord shall send the rod of thy strength out of Zion: rule thou in the midst of thine enemies."

Psalm 110:2 KJV

Day 1

PROPHETIC INSIGHT

As you begin your journey, there will be many levels and forms of resistance. God will anoint you to overcome every force and limitation, in whatever way it presents itself. Apostolically, you have been sent, and the package that you were sent with is your divine ability to overcome anything because the Lord is with you. Therefore, rule right in the midst of opposition.

PROPHETIC INTERCESSION

As you intercede and meditate on the Word of God, take some time to intercede and ponder on the Scripture above. See yourself ruling in the midst of your limitations or opposition. Record what the Lord reveals to you.

Day 1

Day 1

"Behold, the Lord thy God hath set the land before thee: go up and possess it, as the Lord God of thy fathers hath said unto thee; fear not, neither be discouraged."

Deuteronomy 1:21 KJV

Day 2

PROPHETIC INSIGHT

As we commence the development of blazing a trail, we must first scope out the territory that needs cultivation. This is the place where you will not only establish the will of God but create what has never been.

PROPHETIC INTERCESSION

As you intercede and meditate on the Word of God, take some time to receive the blueprint for the territory given unto you. You have been graced with this place to possess it. See yourself as a divine architect and follow the Lord's instructions precisely.

Day 2

Day 2

"And God blessed them, and God said unto them, Be fruitful, and multiply, and replenish the earth, and subdue it: and have dominion over the fish of the sea, and over the fowl of the air, and over every living thing that moveth upon the earth."

Genesis 1:28 KJV

Day 3

PROPHETIC INSIGHT

As we pioneer into this new territory, our divine mandate unfolds: to populate the land with a vibrant community and rich culture. Our calling is to establish a new cultural identity anchored in the apostolic and prophetic foundations, aligning with God's will and purposes. In this endeavor, we must also seek out like-minded individuals who share in our vision.

PROPHETIC INTERCESSION

As you intercede and meditate on the Word of God, envision yourself contributing to the creation of a community with unique innovative abilities. A community of trailblazers and trendsetters who are constantly pushing the boundaries of what is possible, never content with maintaining the status quo, but instead always striving for more.

Day 3

Day 3

"And are built upon the foundation of the apostles and prophets, Jesus Christ himself being the chief corner stone; In whom all the building fitly framed together groweth unto an holy temple in the Lord: In whom ye also are builded together for an habitation of God through the Spirit."

Ephesians 2:20-22 KJV

Day 4

PROPHETIC INSIGHT

Create an atmosphere and develop a culture-climate. Establish a clear vision and mission for this movement grounded in biblical principles and values. Appoint leaders who are apostolic and prophetic, coupled with intercession and humility. With these elements in place, the culture of the movement develops strongly and thrives, making a lasting impact on the world.

PROPHETIC INTERCESSION

As you intercede and meditate on the Word of God, reflect on being a frontliner who has helped establish a community of like-minded people receiving support as they engage in unprecedented endeavors. Record the ideas that the Lord is impressing upon you.

Day 4

Day 4

"According to the grace of God which is given unto me, as a wise masterbuilder, I have laid the foundation, and another buildeth thereon. But let every man take heed how he buildeth thereupon. For other foundation can no man lay than that is laid, which is Jesus Christ. Now if any man build upon this foundation gold, silver, precious stones, wood, hay, stubble; Every man's work shall be made manifest: for the day shall declare it, because it shall be revealed by fire; and the fire shall try every man's work of what sort it is. If any man's work abide which he hath built thereupon, he shall receive a reward. If any man's work shall be burned, he shall suffer loss: but he himself shall be saved; yet so as by fire."

1 Corinthians 3:10-15 KJV

Day 5

PROPHETIC INSIGHT

Form teams out of your population. To build effective teams within a powerful community with different agendas, it is important to first recognize and respect the unique strengths and perspectives of each member. Building on this foundation of diversity and mutual respect, leaders can work to create a shared vision and set goals that everyone can rally around. Communication and collaboration are key in this process, as team members must be able to share their ideas, give and receive feedback, and work together toward common objectives. By fostering an environment of openness, trust, and deep connection, leaders can help individuals within a spiritual movement come together to achieve something truly meaningful and impactful.

PROPHETIC INTERCESSION

As you intercede and meditate on the Word of God, reflect on how you can use your strengths to help achieve the vision and mission of the team that is birthing this movement. Take some time to brainstorm ideas and strategies on how you can use your talents to be a history-maker, making a meaningful impact on those for whom you pave the way.

Day 5

Day 5

"Where there is no vision, the people perish: but he that keepeth the law, happy is he."

Proverbs 29:18 KJV

Day 6

PROPHETIC INSIGHT

Lay a foundation and cast a vision that has never been seen or accomplished. To truly establish this work, it is crucial to lay a solid foundation and cast a clear vision by establishing core values and principles that guide decision-making. This is key so that individuals can lead with excellence. Also, it means fostering a culture of collaboration and shared vision, where everyone is working toward the same goals, supporting each other as a team along the way.

PROPHETIC INTERCESSION

As you intercede and meditate on the Word of God, reflect on ways to effectively communicate the vision and inspire others to join this journey. Consider the most effective ways to share your message with other passionate team members that will birth excitement and momentum.

Day 6

Day 6

"But seek ye first the kingdom of God, and his righteousness; and all these things shall be added unto you."

Matthew 6:33 KJV

Day 7

PROPHETIC INSIGHT

You must seek the Kingdom. This keeps you in sync and time-relevant with the times we are living in. As your mind is renewed, it produces a Kingdom mindset that dictates your Kingdom actions and language. This will result in a powerful manifestation. Therefore, your agenda now becomes the agenda of the Kingdom.

PROPHETIC INTERCESSION

As you intercede and meditate on the Word of God, reflect on how to integrate seeking the Kingdom into your daily decisions and actions. How can you leverage your unique talents and abilities to advance God's Kingdom purposes in the world around you?

Day 7

Day 7

"Praying always with all prayer and supplication in the Spirit, and watching thereunto with all perseverance and supplication for all saints; And for me, that utterance may be given unto me, that I may open my mouth boldly, to make known the mystery of the gospel."

Ephesians 6:18-19 KJV

Day 8

PROPHETIC INSIGHT

There is a realm of intercession that brings interpretation to mysteries in the Kingdom. This level of intercession releases revelation, instruction, and blueprints as you pioneer with a great purpose.

PROPHETIC INTERCESSION

As you intercede and meditate on the Word of God, spend some time in prayer and reflection, asking God to reveal any areas where He may be calling you to deeper levels of intercession. Ask Him to show you how your prayers can release revelation, instruction, and blueprints for this assignment in His Kingdom.

Day 8

Day 8

"I will praise thee; for I am fearfully and wonderfully made: marvellous are thy works; and that my soul knoweth right well."

Psalm 139:14 KJV

Day 9

PROPHETIC INSIGHT

You must have clarification of your identity. Why? Being secure in your identity means knowing your worth and staying true to yourself. This keeps you on course and is a constant reminder of your assignment and its importance.

PROPHETIC INTERCESSION

As you intercede and meditate on the Word of God, spend some time thinking about how you faced obstacles or challenges in the process of pursuing your goal. Notice how you never lost the essence of who you are. You are made in the image and likeness of God.

Day 9

Day 9

"I can do all things through Christ which strengtheneth me."

Philippians 4:13 KJV

Day 10

PROPHETIC INSIGHT

You must deal with any form of insecurity, as you embark on your pioneering journey. Recognize that insecurities may arise. However, trust in the abilities and the guidance of the Lord to help you overcome them.

PROPHETIC INTERCESSION

As you intercede and meditate on the Word of God, reflect on self-care. Ask God to help you see yourself as He sees you. Receive it, be confident, and walk in it.

Day 10

# Day 10

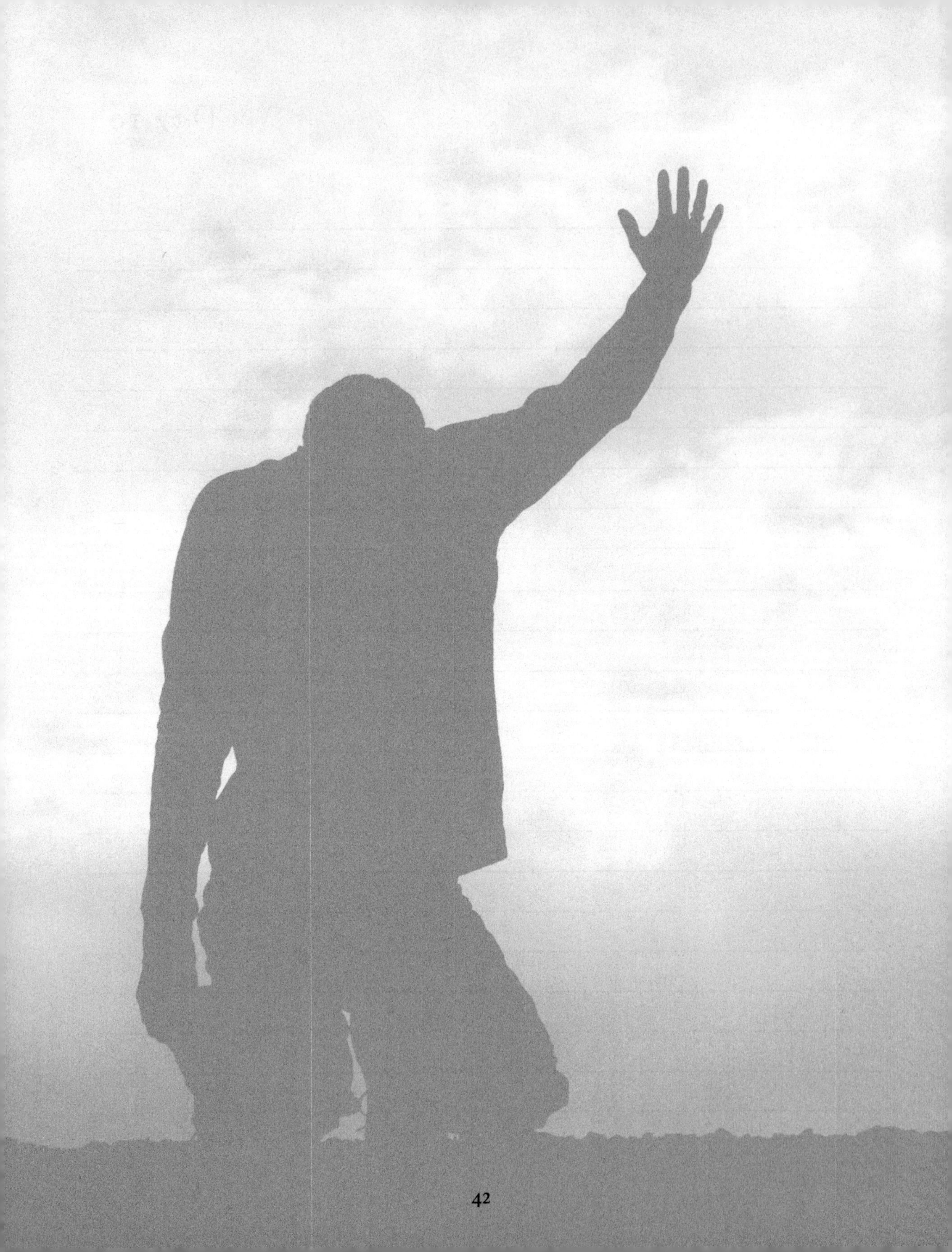

To the trendsetter forging an Apostolic culture of birthing and building, your vision is a beacon of inspiration. Your wisdom in constructing this culture (like a master builder) is evident in every choice you make. Your foundation is unshakable, rooted in timeless values.

You're not just following trends; you're creating a legacy. Your culture nurtures creativity, innovation, and unity. You're not alone in this endeavor, for you inspire others to join in. You're a pioneer, leading by example, and your impact will resonate for generations.

"When thou passest through the waters, I will be with thee; and through the rivers, they shall not overflow thee: when thou walkest through the fire, thou shalt not be burned; neither shall the flame kindle upon thee. For I am the Lord thy God, the Holy One of Israel, thy Saviour: I gave Egypt for thy ransom, Ethiopia and Seba for thee."

Isaiah 43:2-3 KJV

Day 11

PROPHETIC INSIGHT

When high levels of pain and discouragement hit your life, continue to push, and never quit!!! There is an opening in the Spirit. You are close!

PROPHETIC INTERCESSION

As you intercede and meditate on the Word of God, reflect on past challenges that you have overcome. This will give you strength for the present. Remember God's strength is made perfect where you are weak (2 Corinthians 12:9).

Day 11

Day 11

"Blessed are ye, when men shall revile you, and persecute you, and shall say all manner of evil against you falsely, for my sake. Rejoice, and be exceeding glad: for great is your reward in heaven: for so persecuted they the prophets which were before you."

Matthew 5:11-12 KJV

Day 12

PROPHETIC INSIGHT

Due to the nature of those who go first (blazing a trail), remember that religion, tradition, and hell will challenge you. You have been designed for this.

PROPHETIC INTERCESSION

As you intercede and meditate on the Word of God, reflect on the strengths and qualities you possess that make you uniquely equipped to navigate the challenges and discouragement from traditional or cultural norms. Stand true to how God has created you to be.

Day 12

Day 12

"For the earth shall be filled with the knowledge of the glory of the Lord, as the waters cover the sea."

Habakkuk 2:14 KJV

Day 13

PROPHETIC INSIGHT

Begin to birth revival personally and corporately through teaching. Many will need to be revived to function in this time. Bring into perspective that God's glory and power are in control.

PROPHETIC INTERCESSION

As you intercede and meditate on the Word of God, reflect on the areas of your life that need spiritual renewal and revitalization. What steps can you take to invite God's transformation into those areas to bring personal revival? Also, reflect on the state of the church, community, and nation. Think about ways to advocate and bring healing to this land. Let's take bold actions in this season and release the glory of God.

Day 13

Day 13

"Have not I commanded thee? Be strong and of a good courage; be not afraid, neither be thou dismayed: for the Lord thy God is with thee whithersoever thou goest."

Joshua 1:9 KJV

Day 14

PROPHETIC INSIGHT

As you embrace your assignment, the Lord will reveal things to you as you go. Therefore, when you see the fullness of the assignment: FEAR NOT! Jesus will give you the ability to execute.

PROPHETIC INTERCESSION

As you intercede and meditate on the Word of God, think of Daniel's unwavering faith and trust in the Lord. Despite facing potential death, Daniel remained steadfast, praying to his God three times a day. His faithfulness was rewarded, as God sent an angel to protect him from the lions, ultimately leading to the glorification of God. This story challenges us to trust in Christ without fear and to faithfully follow Him, knowing that He can do amazing things in and through us.

Day 14

Day 14

"And be not conformed to this world: but be ye transformed by the renewing of your mind, that ye may prove what is that good, and acceptable, and perfect, will of God."

Romans 12:2 KJV

Day 15

PROPHETIC INSIGHT

This breed of people is a culture that is fearless, positioned with demonstration and power. They flow in the realm of the unorthodox, unpredictable, uncompromising, and unprecedented fueled by grace.

PROPHETIC INTERCESSION

As you intercede and meditate on the Word of God, remember that you are a protagonist embarking on a transformative journey. In a world where you have been chosen for a special mission, you must embrace your God-given assignment, summoning unwavering strength and confidence. Write a compelling story, where fortified by your faith in Jesus, you fearlessly face the challenges ahead. Explore the incredible strength and supernatural abilities that emerge when you wholeheartedly trust in Jesus to empower you in executing your divine purpose. As you navigate the path laid before you, highlight the struggles, triumphs, and moments of profound revelation that shape your character and inspire others to embrace their own assignments with faith and courage.

Day 15

Day 15

"For the earnest expectation of the creature waiteth for the manifestation of the sons of God. For the creature was made subject to vanity, not willingly, but by reason of him who hath subjected the same in hope, Because the creature itself also shall be delivered from the bondage of corruption into the glorious liberty of the children of God. For we know that the whole creation groaneth and travaileth in pain together until now."

Romans 8:19-22 KJV

Day 16

PROPHETIC INSIGHT

When you make a sound, the earth responds to you. The earth has been waiting. In symphony of existence, our voices are notes that resonate with the world around us. Let us be mindful of the sounds we release for each one is part of a dialogue with the patiently awaiting earth.

PROPHETIC INTERCESSION

As you intercede and meditate on the Word of God, think of this as a harmonic convergence, an awakening of the earth's response in which you play a vital part.

Day 16

Day 16

"Through faith we understand that the worlds were framed by the word of God, so that things which are seen were not made of things which do appear"

Hebrews 11:3 KJV

Day 17

PROPHETIC INSIGHT

There is an opening in the earth from every word you speak. Christ makes room for Himself.

PROPHETIC INTERCESSION

As you intercede and meditate on the Word of God, think about this: when we speak prophetic words of faith in obedience, we create a space for God to move mightily in our lives and in the world. It is through our words that God makes room for Himself, as we partner with Him to bring His kingdom into every sphere of influence. Our words become a catalyst for transformation, paving the way for God's glory to be revealed miraculously. In this, we establish the secret things that God has revealed in heaven to come to earth.

Let us use our words wisely, speaking with intention and faith. As we use our words wisely, we become channels for God's divine purpose that ushers His presence into every aspect of our lives.

Day 17

Day 17

And they said one to another, Did not our heart burn within us, while he talked with us by the way, and while he opened to us the scriptures?"

Luke 24:32 KJV

Day 18

PROPHETIC INSIGHT

You will begin to burn with the passion for prayer/intercession in a Holy habitation with the Father. The fire for the trail has been ignited.

PROPHETIC INTERCESSION

As you meditate on the Word of God (prophetic instructions), let it open you up to the transformative power of His truth. In the stillness of contemplation, invite the fire of God to burn brightly within you. Through intercession, yearn for His presence to ignite your spirit with passion and fervency.

In the embrace of God's Word, let Him stir you to action. Allow His truth to stoke the flames of your heart, propelling you to step out in faith, transcend limitations, and explore uncharted territories. The fire within you will compel you to venture into new endeavors and to boldly pursue God's calling on your life.

With each moment spent in His presence, you will kindle a passion that cannot be contained. This passion fuels your dedication and propels you to make a difference. This will empower you to impact the world around you. You are a world-changer.

May the fire of God burn brightly within you. Transcend boundaries and pursue new horizons. In Him, your passion will find its true purpose, and together, there will be a transformation of lives, communities, and beyond.

Day 18

Day 18

"And Moses stretched out his hand over the sea; and the Lord caused the sea to go back by a strong east wind all that night, and made the sea dry land, and the waters were divided. 22 And the children of Israel went into the midst of the sea upon the dry ground: and the waters were a wall unto them on their right hand, and on their left."

Exodus 14:21-22 KJV

Day 19

PROPHETIC INSIGHT

Trends are beginning to form. Forerunners are being released and a fresh move of the Spirit is on the rise. There is fire in your footsteps! This is an Apostolic movement. Just as Moses led the Israelites out of slavery, he was a pioneer of liberation.

PROPHETIC INTERCESSION

As you intercede and meditate on the Word of God, envision a modern parallel– a new movement emerging, marked by pioneers and a fresh outpouring of the Spirit. It's as if there's a blazing trail under your feet. This represents an Apostolic movement. Your task is to craft an engaging narrative or reflection on this contemporary Apostolic movement. Draw connections between the old and the new, and emphasize the role of today's pioneers, who much like Moses, are divinely led, breaking down barriers, and guiding people toward spiritual liberation.

Day 19

Day 19

"One generation shall praise thy works to another, and shall declare thy mighty acts."

Psalm 145:4 KJV

Day 20

PROPHETIC INSIGHT

You have a responsibility to future generations/ there are many standing behind you. You must keep the momentum on this journey because others are depending on you.

PROPHETIC INTERCESSION

As you intercede and meditate on the Word of God, contemplate the broader impact of your actions on future generations beyond your immediate family. How do you envision passing down your knowledge, values, and positive contributions to benefit those who come after you? What steps can you take to ensure that your journey leaves a positive and lasting impact on the generations to come?

Day 20

Day 20

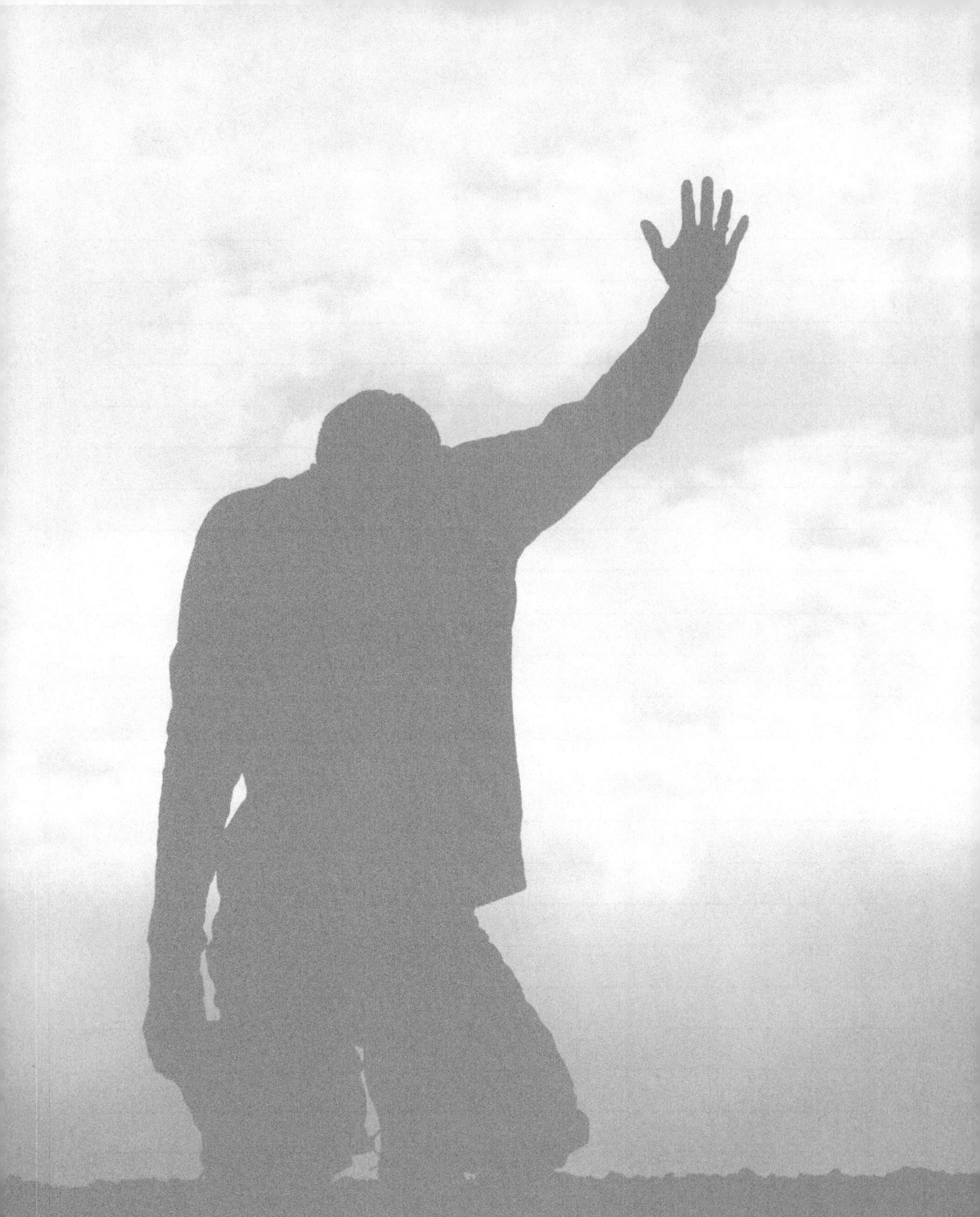

Embrace your uniqueness and be proud to be the first to accomplish great things. Your willingness to pave new paths and innovate sets you apart and inspires others to follow in your footsteps. Trust in God's plan for you as you fearlessly lead the way toward success and fulfillment. You are destined for greatness and to do incredible exploits.

"Behold, I will do a new thing; now it shall spring forth; shall ye not know it? I will even make a way in the wilderness, and rivers in the desert."

Isaiah 43:19 KJV

Day 21

PROPHETIC INSIGHT

You will not be added into paradigms that are no longer effective, but you will be the instrument of change to create the way (the trail).

PROPHETIC INTERCESSION

As you intercede and meditate on the Word of God, reflect on the idea of moving away from paradigms that are no longer effective for you and focus on igniting new paths. How do you feel about embracing change and stepping into unchartered territory? What might the "new thing" that God is doing in your life look like? How can you actively participate in making a way in the wilderness for yourself and others who may be seeking a different path?

Day 21

Day 21

"*God is our refuge and strength, a very present help in trouble.*"

Psalm 46:1 KJV

Day 22

PROPHETIC INSIGHT

Take care of yourself while completing your assignment. Reflect on Him and remain prayerful to keep your strength and confidence strong.

PROPHETIC INTERCESSION

As you intercede and meditate on the Word of God, reflect on how you can implement a routine of prayer and fasting to maintain strength, focus, and tenacity.

Day 22

Day 22

"Then the Spirit said unto Philip, Go near, and join thyself to this chariot."

Acts 8:29 KJV

Day 23

PROPHETIC INSIGHT

Always respond to the instruction and swift movement of Holy Spirit. He leads you into places that need His truth.

PROPHETIC INTERCESSION

As you intercede and meditate on the Word of God, reflect on the idea of always responding to the instruction and swift movement of the Holy Spirit, while trusting that He leads you into places that need His truth. Have there been moments in your life when you felt a strong inner prompting or conviction to take action? How did you respond, and what were the outcomes? Consider how you can become more attuned to the guidance of the Holy Spirit in your daily life and the impact it can have on sharing truth and love with those around you.

Day 23

Day 23

"Go ye therefore, and teach all nations, baptizing them in the name of the Father, and of the Son, and of the Holy Ghost: Teaching them to observe all things whatsoever I have commanded you: and, lo, I am with you always, even unto the end of the world. Amen."

Matthew 28:19-20 KJV

Day 24

PROPHETIC INSIGHT

You must have a burden for missions and the masses to develop and train others to take and create territories. This is an apostolic work.

PROPHETIC INTERCESSION

As you intercede and meditate on the Word of God, reflect on the concept of having a burden for missions and the masses, as well as the responsibility to develop and train others to expand and impact territories. What does this idea mean to you personally, and how does it align with your values and beliefs? Consider how you can take on an apostolic role in your own life, whether in a religious or secular context, to inspire and equip others for meaningful and impactful work.

Day 24

Day 24

"For we are his workmanship, created in Christ Jesus unto good works, which God hath before ordained that we should walk in them."

Ephesians 2:10 KJV

Day 25

PROPHETIC INSIGHT

Today, you will begin to sense the power of your calling to change societal, economic, and global issues. You are a world changer blazing something new.

PROPHETIC INTERCESSION

As you intercede and meditate on the Word of God, reflect on the idea that today, you are beginning to sense the power of your calling to effect change. What does it mean to you to be a catalyst for positive change on such a scale? How do you envision your unique gifts and abilities contributing to this mission? Consider the steps you can take today to align your actions with your calling and make a meaningful impact on the world.

Day 25

Day 25

"He is like a man which built an house, and digged deep, and laid the foundation on a rock: and when the flood arose, the stream beat vehemently upon that house, and could not shake it: for it was founded upon a rock."

Luke 6:48 KJV

Day 26

PROPHETIC INSIGHT

A new foundation has been established by your obedience. Ponder on your forward movement and look at what has been established thus far.

PROPHETIC INTERCESSION

As you intercede and meditate on the Word of God, reflect on the new foundation being established through your obedience. Consider how far you have come and what has been built as a result. What challenges or obstacles have you faced along the way, and how have they tested the strength of this foundation? Take some time to appreciate the progress you've made and the growth you've experienced along your journey of obedience. What are your hopes and goals for the future as you continue to build upon this foundation?

Day 26

Day 26

"Be ye followers of me, even as
I also am of Christ."

1 Corinthians 11:1 KJV

Day 27

PROPHETIC INSIGHT

Reproduce after the model Jesus has given to you. Obedience and execution for this model is crucial.

PROPHETIC INTERCESSION

As you intercede and meditate on the Word of God, reflect on the different aspects of Jesus' life, teachings, and character. What do you find most inspiring and worth emulating?

Day 27

Day 27

"And the Lord shall utter his voice before his army: for his camp is very great: for he is strong that executeth his word: for the day of the Lord is great and very terrible; and who can abide it?"

Joel 2:11 KJV

Day 28

PROPHETIC INSIGHT

Look around you. Survey your surroundings. Witness the formidable force of Believers, steadfast and ready for whatever comes their way.

PROPHETIC INTERCESSION

As you intercede and meditate on the Word of God, reflect on the challenges and uncertainties you may be facing in your life right now. How can you draw strength, support, and inspiration from the presence of fellow believers who stand with you? Consider the power of unity and shared faith in facing life's battles together (destiny helpers).

Day 28

Day 28

"So that ye come behind in no gift; waiting for the coming of our Lord Jesus Christ."

1 Corinthians 1:7 KJV

Day 29

PROPHETIC INSIGHT

Your gift holds a significant role in the grand scheme of ushering the second coming of Christ. This contributes to the fulfillment of divine purpose and the realization of God's kingdom on Earth.

PROPHETIC INTERCESSION

As you intercede and meditate on the Word of God, reflect on what you believe your unique gifts and talents are, and how can you use them to contribute to the greater mission of preparing for Christ's return. How does this sense of purpose and responsibility impact your daily life and the choices you make? Consider the ways in which you can actively participate in fulfilling this calling and the significance it holds for your faith journey.

Day 29

Day 29

"Ye are the light of the world. A city that is set on an hill cannot be hid. Neither do men light a candle, and put it under a bushel, but on a candlestick; and it giveth light unto all that are in the house. Let your light so shine before men, that they may see your good works, and glorify your Father which is in heaven."

Matthew 5:14-16 KJV

Day 30

PROPHETIC INSIGHT

The trail is on fire ignited with fervor; the Kingdom has been released and you emerge as a pivotal figure in shaping history.

PROPHETIC INTERCESSION

As you intercede and meditate on the Word of God, reflect on the statement: "The Kingdom has been released and you emerge as a pivotal figure in shaping history."

How does this idea make you feel, and what does it mean to you personally to be part of something so significant? Consider the ways in which you can let your light shine before others and contribute to the advancement of God's Kingdom in your own unique way.

Day 30

Day 30

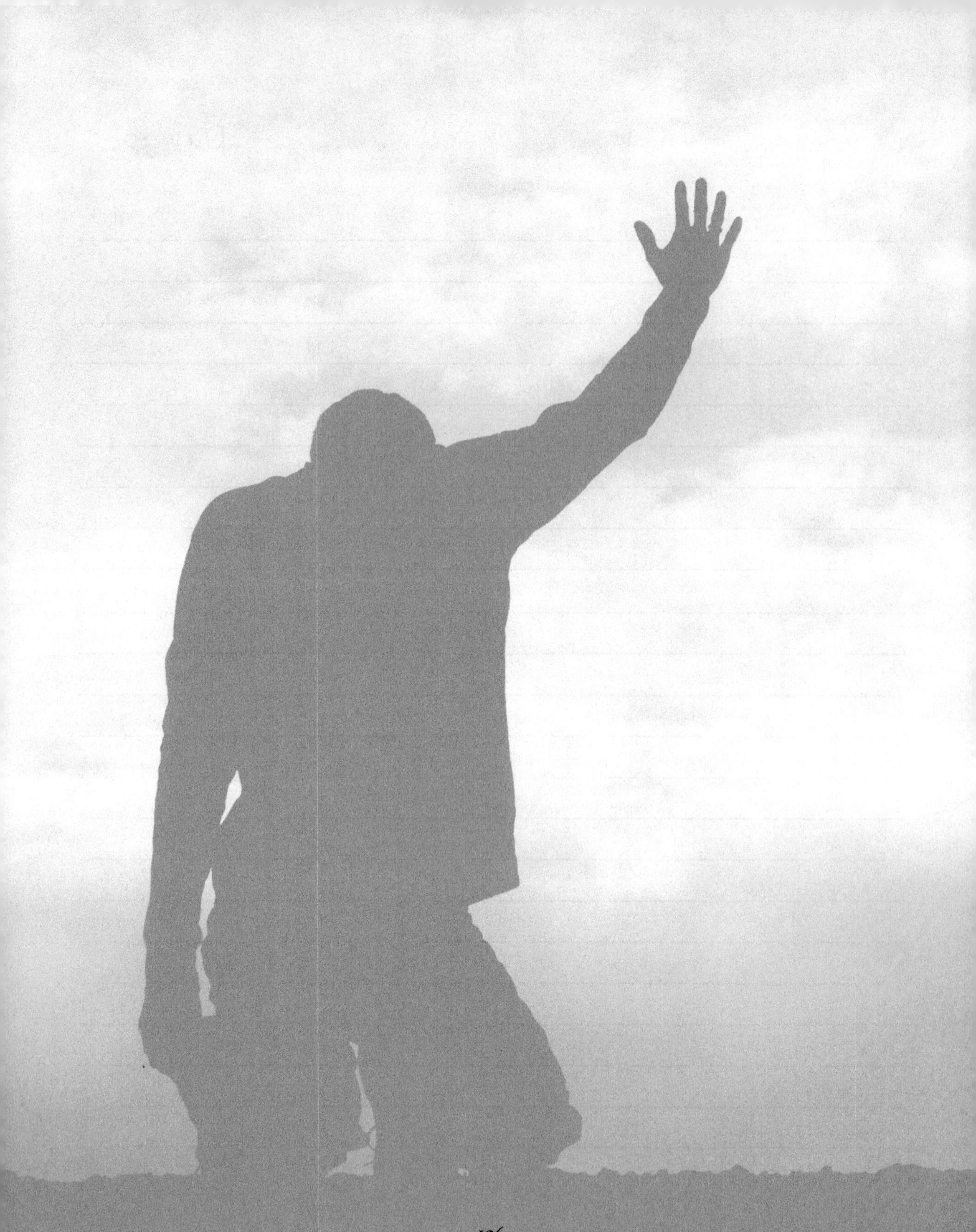

To the trailblazers, the 'sent ones' carrying a movement that births personal and corporate revival and restoration, you are pioneers of an unprecedented journey. Your path is a beacon of hope, igniting fires of transformation in individuals, communities, nations, and regions. As reformers, your movement is a unique blaze, forging a trail where none has ventured before. Celebrate your extraordinary mission and the global legacy you are creating.

I declare and pray for every pioneer who reads this book and those who will come across this prayer.

May they keep the momentum and overcome every oppositional force.

May they be blessed with the courage and strength to blaze new trails and accomplish remarkable feats.

May their actions be a prophetic demonstration of God's grace, leading to incredible manifestations and blessings.

May they inspire others to follow in their footsteps and achieve greatness.

In Jesus' Name,
Amen.

ABOUT THE AUTHOR

Rhonda R. Bratcher is the founder of Frontline Warriors for Christ International Ministry Inc., an apostolic and prophetic ministry in Baltimore, MD. She is an Apostle who is called to be a Kingdom voice that reforms leaders and regions by unveiling God's truth. She is a deeply passionate prophetic intercessor, revivalist, and teacher of the Word of God who operates strongly in deliverance, healing, and worship. Her mandate is to equip the saints by building and releasing strong apostolic ministry teams of intercessors, healers, deliverers, apostles, and prophets who understand spiritual warfare and culture which advances the purposes of the Kingdom of God. She is supported by her husband Rodney Bratcher Sr., her three beautiful children (Anthony, Kaine, and Rodney Jr.), and her four grandchildren (Kamryn, Kyla, Rodney, and Kash).

Made in the USA
Middletown, DE
07 April 2024